Bonjour, Là, Bonjour

BONJOUR, LA, BONJOUR

MICHEL TREMBLAY

Talonbooks • Vancouver • 1988

copyright ©1988 Michel Tremblay

translation copyright ©1988 John Van Burek and Bill Glassco

published with assistance from the Canada Council

Talonbooks
201/1019 East Cordova Street
Vancouver, British Columbia
Canada V6A 1M8

This book was typeset in Garth by Pièce de Résistance Graphics, and printed by Hignell Printing Ltd.

Printed in Canada

First revised printing: October 1988

First published by Les Editions Leméac Inc., Montréal, Québec.

Canadian Cataloguing in Publication Data

Tremblay, Michel, 1943-
  [Bonjour, là, bonjour. English]
  Bonjour, là, bonjour

  Translation of: Bonjour, là, bonjour.
  ISBN 0-88922-252-5

  I. Title. II. Title: Bonjour, là, bonjour.
  English.
  PS8539.R47B613 1988   C842'.54   C88-091494-7
  PQ3919.2.T73B613 1988

Bonjour, là, Bonjour was first performed by the Compagnie des Deux Chaises at the National Art Centre in Ottawa, Ontario, on August 22, 1974, with the following cast:

Lucienne	Denise Pelletier
Denise	Amulette Garneau
Monique	Monique Joly
Nicole	Odette Gagnon
Albertine	Rita Lafontaine
Charlotte	Frédérique Collin
Gabriel	Gilles Renaud
Serge	Guy Thauvette

Directed by André Brassard
Designed by Guy Neveu
Costumes by François Laplante

This revised version of *Bonjour, là, Bonjour* was first performed in English at CentreStage in Toronto, Ontario on November 25, 1986, with the following cast:

Armand	Donald Davis
Gilberte	Marion Gilsenan
Charlotte	Joyce Campion
Serge	Stephen Ouimette
Lucienne	Shirley Douglas
Denise	Diane Douglass
Monique	Nancy Beatty
Nicole	Deborah Grover

Directed by François Barbeau
Set designed by André Hénault
Costumes designed by Sylvain Labelle
Lighting designed by Sholem Dolgoy
Sound designed by Nick Name

No. 1 Trio

ARMAND:
So, how did you like Europe?

GILBERTE:
Your aunty would have loved that, to go away on trips.

CHARLOTTE:
You know what your aunty's always dreamed of? To take a trip around the world.

ARMAND:
Is it as nice as everyone says?

GILBERTE & CHARLOTTE:
But no, your aunty was never that lucky.

ARMAND:
You know what, you're a lucky fellow. The first one in the family to cross the Atlantic.

GILBERTE:
No he's not . . .

1

ARMAND:

Sure, your uncle Fernand during the war, but when he got there it was all over. They just turned him around and shipped him back.

CHARLOTTE:

No, aunty was never that lucky.

ARMAND:

He never got past London and that's only England. Never had time. Nope, you're the first.

GILBERTE:

Were you sick to your stomach on the plane?

ARMAND:

That's what I was telling the boys at the tavern the other day. I said, "My Serge is the first one in the family to spend three whole months in Europe."

CHARLOTTE:

Three months . . . Well, aunty could spend three years far from this place.

ARMAND:

I bought them a round and I told them everything you said in your letters. Oh they probably heard it before, but when I buy, they listen. They know what I've got to say is important, even if they heard it before . . . And if any of them don't want to listen, Bonnier just tells them to shut up and he goes over and turns off the television. So I stood up and I told them everything you said in your letters from Greece.

GILBERTE:

Must be long, eh, seven hours on the plane?

CHARLOTTE:

They say Paris is shaped like an onion. Is that true?

ARMAND:
> You should have seen the look on their faces.
> They're a nice bunch of guys all right, but they
> don't know anything. Never been further than Guy
> and Dorchester. You mention St-Lambert, they don't
> know what you're talking about. There's a couple of
> young snots in there too, who didn't want to believe
> me. Seems they started shouting, "Water that blue?
> Impossible! Sit down, Armand, you're making it
> up." Of course me, I couldn't hear them. Hell,
> Bonnier had to show them the stamp on the
> envelope before they'd shut up.

CHARLOTTE:
> Be honest now, is the water really that blue?

GILBERTE:
> Charlotte, if Serge said so . . .

ARMAND:
> They're just jealous, the whole bunch of 'em. Never
> done a thing since the day they were born and
> probably never will. Of course when it's time to
> criticize, they know everything. Do they ever. Even
> when it isn't time. They loaf around the tavern all
> day, make fun of everyone else, but you think
> they'd lift a finger to go out and earn some money?
> Not on your life. I tell those young buggers all the
> time, and you know me, I don't mince words.
> "You're not even twenty-five," I tell them, "and
> here you are acting like me, a retired man. Is this
> tomorrow's future generation? Come on, get off
> your asses! You go on like this, you won't amount to
> a thing. Go on like this, you won't even get a wife.
> And those of you who got wives, I hope you buy
> some lifesavers before you go home, because you
> smell like cows." You know what one of them told
> me once? Screamed it right in my face to make sure
> I'd understand. "Me," he says, "I drink my beer
> here and the old lady drinks hers at home. So we
> got no problem with bad breath." It's times like
> that, I'm sorry I can read lips . . .

3

GILBERTE:
    Must be quite a change, eh, to live in a different
    country with people you don't even know?

CHARLOTTE:
    Of course silly old me, every morning I'd go
    downstairs to see if there wasn't a letter.

GILBERTE:
    Must be hard to get used to, eh?

CHARLOTTE:
    As if you had time to write every day! You don't
    even phone us when you're here, why would you
    write every day from Europe?

GILBERTE:
    You're gonna laugh, but you know what? Every
    time they showed a French movie on television, I
    thought of you. And I'd ask myself, "How in the
    world does he manage?"

CHARLOTTE:
    Sometimes when we didn't hear for a while your
    father got pretty worried . . .

ARMAND:
    But here I'm doing all the talking and you're the one
    who's just come home . . .

CHARLOTTE:
    Sometimes when we didn't hear for a while your
    father got pretty worried . . . .

GILBERTE:
    All right, Charlotte, we heard you the first time!

CHARLOTTE:
    Well, he wasn't listening! Nobody ever listens to
    me.

GILBERTE:
> If nobody listens to you it's 'cause you're a bore.

CHARLOTTE:
> And what makes you think you're so interesting?

ARMAND:
> Are the European girls pretty?

GILBERTE & CHARLOTTE:
> Are the European girls pretty?

GILBERTE:
> We thought you might come home with a girl from Paris.

CHARLOTTE:
> Oh, that would have surprised me . . .

GILBERTE:
> That would have surprised you, would it?

CHARLOTTE:
> Of course it would.

GILBERTE:
> And why, might I ask?

CHARLOTTE:
> I've got my reasons . . .

GILBERTE:
> Aren't you the clever one . . .

CHARLOTTE:
> Look, I've got my reasons!

GILBERTE:
> Always smarter than the rest of us, aren't you?

CHARLOTTE:
> I didn't say I was smarter. I said it would have surprised me, that's all.

GILBERTE:
> Mind you, you're probably right. Serge has better taste than that.

ARMAND:
> I knew one once. Oh that was a long time ago, before your mother. A Belgian girl. That was way back in the twenties. In those days there weren't so many immigrants as they got now. She wasn't all that pretty, but she was interesting to talk to. That was a long time before . . . my accident. I never would have married her though. Oh no! I don't know how they do it, those people who marry foreigners. But you know, she used to tell me about all the trouble they had over there. It's hard to believe, eh? War, famine . . .
> Everything's happened to those people. They've been through it all. You know, when you stop to think about it, we've got no right to complain. Over here, we've got it good.

CHARLOTTE:
> Not that good!

ARMAND:
> Mind you, that was a long time ago. Maybe things are better now.

GILBERTE:
> How come you don't eat? Your plate's been sitting there for five minutes. You haven't touched it . . . I thought you liked roast beef.

CHARLOTTE:
> Maybe it's too rare. He likes it well done, you know.

GILBERTE:
Oh that's right. I forgot you liked the outside. Good
Lord, the things you forget in three months . . .

CHARLOTTE:
Would you like your Aunt Charlotte to change your
plate? Here, I'll get you some more peas too.

GILBERTE:
Maybe I should warm up the potatoes . . .

ARMAND:
You can tell me about Paris, you know. It's true,
I've never been there, but I've read a lot. I've read
all about that stuff. I got the whole map of Paris
right here in my noggin. Your old man's not stupid
you know. Maybe I've never been past Guy and
Dorchester either, but I've kept up with lots of
things. You know the Tour Eiffel? I can tell you
where it is. It's on the Left Bank. And Notre Dame,
I know where that is too. It's on the Ile de la Cité.
Victor Hugo talked so much about that in his book.
You know, when I was out of work during the
Depression, I used to read all kinds of things. You
wouldn't remember that 'cause you weren't born
then, but ask Lucienne. Maupassant and all those
things. I read them all.

GILBERTE:
Maybe he's tired. Maybe he doesn't want to tell us
everything now.

ARMAND:
What?

GILBERTE: *louder*
I said, maybe he's tired. He can tell us about it
another time.

ARMAND:
Come on! A son's too tired to talk to his father? We
haven't seen each other for three months. We got
such an earful about this trip before he left, don't
tell me he's got nothing to say now that he's back.
Besides, you told me yourself at Dorval that because
of the time change, you've got to stay awake at least
until midnight. So go ahead, shoot, I'm listening.

GILBERTE:
Let him eat, Armand, he can tell us about it later.

No. 2 Duet

SERGE: *too loudly, articulating too much so that his
father will understand him*
Yeah, Paris is really beautiful! It's a . . . fabulous
city. It's big. Er . . . Wherever you go it's beautiful. I
mean, there are no ugly places. At least I didn't see
any.   *louder*   I said I didn't see any place in
Paris that wasn't beautiful. And it's true, the
Seine . . . it's not very wide.   *trying to be
funny*   It looks more like a duck pond than a
river . . .

      Silence.

Er . . . When it's all lit up at night, you know, the
Louvre and all that, it's unbelievable. I thought
about you a lot when I was out walking.   *louder.*
I said, I thought about you when I was out walking,
how you love to take walks. And I knew you'd have
liked it there. You don't realize it at the time, but
you walk for hours and hours. You never get bored.
There's always something interesting to see. What's
really fun is to see the names of streets, they remind
you of so many things. Books, movies, songs . . .
Even the street corners are nice 'cause they're not at

right angles like they are here. There are always five or six streets that come together in the same place so sometimes the streets don't even have corners.

GILBERTE:
I don't think he hears you, Serge. His hearing aid is broken. He's too proud to tell you.

No. 3 Octet

We can hear LUCIENNE laughing before the lights come up on her. The actress should bear in mind that in the original, LUCIENNE speaks in French with a slight English accent as though she has lost the habit of speaking her mother tongue.

LUCIENNE:
Well, if nothing else, did they show you how to live. My God, with hair that long . . . I guess you haven't changed much. Come on, why don't you get it cut? It's not even in style any more. Even Bobby cuts his now and he's only sixteen.

SERGE:
How is Bobby? Still the family bum?

CHARLOTTE:
Lucienne phoned. She wants you to go and see her.

GILBERTE:
She spoke to your Aunt Charlotte. Didn't even ask how I was.

LUCIENNE:
Bobby? Oh his father's right, he'll straighten out. It's his age. Kids always do crazy things at his age. He'll be fine.

SERGE:
   And the girl he knocked up, will she be fine too?

LUCIENNE:
   Look, if you've come here to lecture me again . . . I
   don't need you telling me how to raise my kids.

SERGE:
   Lucienne, I came because you asked me to.

LUCIENNE:
   And you wouldn't have come if I hadn't?

SERGE:
   No, I wouldn't.

LUCIENNE:
   Then why did you bother?

SERGE:
   I thought it might be important since you took the
   trouble to phone me at Papa's . . .

LUCIENNE:
   I didn't want you running straight to Nicole. We'd
   never see you again.

   MONIQUE appears.

MONIQUE:
   Well, Ducky, you finally made it! I've been waiting
   for you for two hours. Hey, before you take off your
   jacket, would you mind going to the drugstore for
   me?

LUCIENNE:
   Are you moving back to her place?

SERGE:
   Her place is my place.

10

NICOLE tries to say something but without success.

LUCIENNE:
> Hey, turn off the stereo, it's giving me a headache.
> I want to talk to you . . . seriously. The first button
> on the left . . . It's new, did you notice? No, of
> course not, you never notice things like that . . .

SERGE:
> What do you mean? Of course I noticed . . .

LUCIENNE:
> Well, you might have said something. It cost me a
> thousand bucks.

SERGE:
> Look, I'm not a kid any more, I'm not going to do
> handstands every time you buy a salad bowl.
> I noticed your new bar too, but I didn't say anything
> 'cause I think a bar in the corner of a living room is
> ugly and yours really takes the cake.

LUCIENNE:
> You're getting jealous . . . just like the others . . .

DENISE appears.

DENISE:
> Well, well, well, surprise, surprise! Come in! Guess
> what, I've got a roast beef in the oven. How's that
> grab you? Here, give us a kiss, a big juicy kiss.

SERGE:
> Look, if you're going to start that again, I'm going
> home to bed. I'm too tired . . .

LUCIENNE:
> No, no, stay here. Stay. Stay the night if you like.
> You can sleep in the guest room. You know we had
> it re-done since you left? I got tired of the Colonial.
> It looked cheap . . .

11

SERGE:
It was me who told you that . . .

LUCIENNE:
So we bought Spanish. It's gorgeous.

Silence.

You'll love it. We put the Colonial in the basement
for Bobby and his friends.

Silence.

So, you had a good trip. Tell me about it . . .

MONIQUE:
How much do I owe you?

SERGE:
Forget it . . .

MONIQUE:
Don't be silly, you're not going to pay for my pills.
Wow . . . They're more expensive than I
thought . . .
I can't afford these too often . . .

LUCIENNE:
I suppose you've just told Papa all about it and you
don't feel like starting over . . .

SERGE:
Lucienne, have you forgotten how we parted three
months ago?

LUCIENNE:
So that's it . . . You're still mad.

MONIQUE:
And there's only twelve of them? Are they crazy?

LUCIENNE:
Even after three months . . .

MONIQUE:
Bob told me I'd have enough for a month!

SERGE:
Maybe you're not supposed to take them every day . . .

LUCIENNE:
Okay, so I got a little drunk that night . . . and you don't like it when people get drunk.

SERGE:
I don't mind if people drink provided they don't bawl me out and provided they don't throw up all over my plate.

LUCIENNE:
Serge, I don't remember everything I did, but I certainly did not throw up all over your plate.

SERGE:
Okay, okay, let's not get into that tonight . . . I've got other people to see . . .

MONIQUE:
If things keep going the way they are, I'll take the whole bottle, and then . . .

SERGE:
Bye, bye.

MONIQUE:
Bye, bye, world.

LUCIENNE:
Look, I asked you to stay . . . I have something important to tell you.

GILBERTE & CHARLOTTE:
>Your father ran into your sister Lucienne on la rue
>Ste-Catherine the other day . . .

ARMAND:
>I ran into your sister Lucienne on la rue
>Ste-Catherine the other day.

GILBERTE & CHARLOTTE:
>Your father ran into your sister Lucienne on la rue
>Ste-Catherine the other day and . . .

SERGE:
>Okay, what is it this time?

GILBERTE & CHARLOTTE:
>She was with another man . . .

MONIQUE:
>For a while I stopped taking them altogether . . . I
>felt better too. But now . . . now I get these funny
>sensations . . .

LUCIENNE:
>I know it sounds funny . . .

DENISE:
>It's funny, I'd forgotten you were so tall.

MONIQUE:
>I'm so feverish lately . . .

DENISE:
>Must be those stupid boots, eh, with the high
>heels . . .

MONIQUE:
>Sometimes I feel fine you know, then all of a
>sudden I get dizzy. I can't see straight. It's scary.

DENISE:
Holy Moses, little brother, are you good looking!

MONIQUE:
It was Bob who gave me the prescription. They're supposed to be good, but he says they're pretty strong.

DENISE:
Come on, sexy, don't stand there in the door. Come in and sit down. You're giving me hot flashes!

NICOLE tries again to say something but without success.

LUCIENNE:
You know things aren't too hot between Bob and me. We've been married twenty years . . . Well, we know all about that. Bonjour, bonjour. Bonsoir, bonsoir. That's about it. Small talk, you know what I mean?

SERGE:
Nothing new about that.

LUCIENNE:
Well . . . I've met someone . . .

SERGE:
That's fine.

LUCIENNE:
Is that all you can say?

SERGE:
If you're happy, I'm happy for you.

LUCIENNE:
There's one problem.

SERGE:
I figured as much.

LUCIENNE:
Will you listen to me . . . Will you let me explain?
It's not easy to say . . .

GILBERTE & CHARLOTTE:
Some young fella . . .

LUCIENNE:
He's your age . . .

GILBERTE:
It's disgusting. A mother with a family!

CHARLOTTE:
That's what you call a pig!

ARMAND:
I pretended not to see her. I didn't want to
embarrass her. But I think she saw me. As she
walked by, she looked in a store window. I think
you know him too . . .

LUCIENNE:
And you know him.

SERGE:
And I even know him! Hey, this story's getting
better all the time. When you tell me his name, I
suppose I'll jump up and say, "Not him, it can't be
him!"

ARMAND:
It's that tall guy you used to bring home all the
time . . . You know, the one who looked like
you . . . The painter. Always smelled like
Varsol . . .

SERGE:
Robert?   *laughing*   Not him, it can't be him!

LUCIENNE:
   It's your friend Robert.

SERGE:
   I know.

LUCIENNE:
   So Papa did see me on the street the other day?

SERGE:
   You got it!

LUCIENNE:
   Shit! Shit! Shit! Shit! . . . What are you laughing at?

SERGE:
   You're married to a Bob, you've got a kid named
   Bobby and out of all my friends you had to pick one
   named Robert.

LUCIENNE:
   Sure, to you it's a joke.

DENISE:
   If I don't control myself, I'm gonna rape you on the
   spot.

SERGE:
   So control yourself.

DENISE:
   After three months? When I dream about you every
   night?

SERGE:
   Here Denise, have some peanuts.

LUCIENNE:
   That's all you've got to say?

SERGE:

Look, I don't care about your sordid affairs. Sleep with whoever you like. If it thaws you out a bit, so much the better.

LUCIENNE:

This is not sordid. It's serious.

SERGE:

Oh for Chrissake, open your eyes. That's Robert's specialty, shacking up with women who could pass for his mother. Whatever happens, don't take him seriously. Have your fun and when it's over, forget him. Just don't make a Greek tragedy out of it. I'm not in the mood.

DENISE & MONIQUE:

Have you been to Lady Westmount's?

LUCIENNE:

How dare you talk to me like that. I won't have it! I'm the one who brought you up and . . .

SERGE:

Lucienne, please! If you asked me to come here it's because you want someone to talk to, anyone, and it's not because you brought me up that . . .

LUCIENNE:

Okay, but can't you see, I don't know what to do any more?

SERGE:

Don't play games with me. You're supposed to be the smart one in the family, the tough one, the one who's made it. You're trying to tell me you don't know what to do? You're telling me you want to drop everything for Robert? Come on! You'd never leave all this to go hole up in a basement with a guy who stinks of paint. I know you better than that. Look, you're married to a doctor, an Anglais on top

18

of that, you've got a seventy thousand dollar house in Cartierville, a charming son who's started to knock up the neighbourhood girls, and two lovely teenage twins who flatly refuse to learn French because their father speaks nothing but English. Now how could you leave all that, Lucienne? You love it too much.

DENISE:
Is Lady Westmount still unhappy, even with all her money?

MONIQUE:
Does she still have her rich-lady problems?

DENISE & MONIQUE:
Did she manage to make you feel sorry for her?

NICOLE:
Are you going to come back and stay with me?

SERGE throws himself into NICOLE's arms. They embrace for a long time.

SERGE:
Yes! . . . Yes! . . . Yes!

NICOLE:
I missed you so much.

SERGE:
Me too . . .

DENISE:
Why don't you take a shower, sexy? You can walk around in your underpants, I'll lose weight just looking at you.

LUCIENNE:
I thought you'd help me work this out, but no, you stand there and laugh at me.

19

NICOLE and SERGE separate.

DENISE:
> Okay, enough of this nonsense. Down to serious
> business. Come on little brother, let's eat. It's awful,
> you know, I'm getting to be such a pig. Every year
> it gets worse.

SERGE:
> Where's Gaston? Isn't he home?

DENISE:
> His bowling, dear, have you forgotten his bowling?
> My life depends on his gutter balls. No kidding, it's
> been that way for fifteen years. Come on, I've got
> boiled potatoes or baked potatoes. What's your
> preference?

SERGE:
> I'm not hungry, I already ate at Papa's.

DENISE:
> Why didn't you wait to eat here? Gilberte can't cook
> to save her life. Especially a roast. The last time I
> went there for supper I could have used an axe.

LUCIENNE:
> Listen to me, dammit!

DENISE:
> Is that what you had, roast beef?

SERGE:
> Yes . . .

DENISE:
> And you didn't need an axe?

SERGE:
> It would have helped . . .

DENISE:
Well, there you are . . .

SERGE:
But what difference does it make?

DENISE:
What difference does it make? Don't you care about eating?

MONIQUE:
It all came back to me while you were gone, Serge, everything I'd been scared of . . . I thought it was over and done with, but . . .

SERGE:
Did you tell your husband about it?

MONIQUE:
I didn't tell anyone. I don't want them to put me away.

SERGE:
They're not going to put you away . . .

MONIQUE:
That's what you think. They watch me all the time. Sometimes in the morning, when I'm not feeling well, you should see the look on their faces. They're just waiting for me to crack.

SERGE:
You'd solve half the problem if you'd get rid of your mother-in-law. I've told you a hundred times.

LUCIENNE:
I want you to listen!

DENISE:
Not even a little slice of well done? It's the outside, you know. Your favourite . . . No? You sure?

No. 4 Quartet

LUCIENNE:
It's true, I've got everything I ever dreamed of. I told myself I wasn't going to end up like Mama, with nothing. I made sure that wouldn't happen to me.

SERGE:
Here we go again, Lucienne in "The Edge of Night."

MONIQUE:
Did Lady Westmount start on Mama again?

LUCIENNE:
I wasn't going to marry some French-Canadian turd who'd give me kids with complexes. Oh no, I was aiming higher than that. I wanted to be on the right side of the tracks, the money side, and that's where I am.

DENISE:
To complain like that on a full stomach. It's almost indecent.

LUCIENNE:
I got what I wanted, I got my Anglais. I went out with Bob for eight years before we got married.

SERGE:
Yeah, yeah, we know all that . . .

LUCIENNE:
I made up my mind I was going to marry him and I did. If I had to wait till he finished school and set up his office, then I'd wait.

DENISE:
She's been going on like that for months. It's ridiculous . . . She must have nothing else to do . . .

LUCIENNE:
When we went out together, I'd pay because I was earning the money. But I didn't care. I didn't care because I knew that someday he'd pay it all back, that he'd pay me back even more than that. Because I knew that someday he'd make big money!

SERGE:
Yeah, yeah, sure . . .

LUCIENNE:
Well, my God, big money isn't the word for it . . . As for kids, I wanted two but we had three. The only mistake in our whole life. Instead of having one the second time, we had two.

MONIQUE:
And her twins, are they still nervous wrecks?

DENISE:
Did you see the little monsters?

LUCIENNE:
Everything else is exactly the way we planned it.

SERGE & LUCIENNE:
We started out at the bottom of the ladder and we climbed, step by step . . .

LUCIENNE:
It took us twenty years, but our dreams have all come true. How do you like that, eh? Well, kiddo, if you only knew. I'm not even forty-five and already my life works like a clock. And that's what they call "having your dreams come true."

DENISE:
The last time I called her she told me she felt like a clock or something . . . She's off her rocker, that one . . .

MONIQUE:
And people tell me I'm off my rocker!

LUCIENNE:
It gets to the point there's nothing left to do. You sit there day in and day out while your life goes by without you and you don't know what to do. To pass the time you go out and buy things, then you stick them in the basement because they're too big . . . Or you sit and watch your kids grow up. Me, I couldn't care less about watching my kids grow up. I'm not interested in children. Never have been.

MONIQUE:
With a doctor for a husband she could have all the pills she wants.

LUCIENNE:
I don't know, sometimes I wonder if I even love my kids. But what's the difference, they love their father more than me. He's the hero. He's the one who started out with nothing, he's the one who's made it. Well, I've got . . . what, twenty-five, thirty years left? And already I know everything that's going to happen to me.

SERGE:
So to fight the boredom you run after young studs . . .

LUCIENNE:
You're so stupid, so stupid. My God, are you stupid!

No. 5 Octet

SERGE:
Lucienne, how many times have we been through this? How many times have you asked me to come all the way out here because you had something

important to tell me when all you really want to tell me is how boring your life is and why I should feel sorry for you? Find something to do if you're so bored. Okay, granted, you've found something to do, but I'll tell you this, going to bed with my friend Robert is not going to solve your problems. He's the dullest guy I ever met.

GILBERTE:
I still can't get over it . . .

SERGE:
And please don't tell me you're in love with him, either.

GILBERTE:
. . . a girl in her position.

SERGE:
You can fuck yourselves black and blue for all I care. Just cut the soap opera.

LUCIENNE:
Look, I've told you, I won't have that language in my house.

SERGE:
Oooh, the doctor's wife rides again . . .

CHARLOTTE:
A doctor's wife . . .

ARMAND:
What in the world is wrong with her?

SERGE: *laughing*
Oh, that . . .

MONIQUE:
The last time I went to see Bob, he almost laughed in my face. You know what he told me? To take my pills and don't think.

SERGE:
Go see someone else . . .

GILBERTE:
That must be why she doesn't phone us any more.
She's too ashamed. And your poor father, he's aged
ten years since he saw her with that bum. No. If
you're a lady, you act like a lady!

ARMAND:
I can't believe she'd ruin her life for nothing. She's
worked so hard.

SERGE:
Don't worry, Papa. *louder* I said, don't
worry. It's not that serious!

ARMAND:
Are you going to go and see her?

SERGE:
It won't do any good . . .

ARMAND:
Of course it will! I can't go, she won't listen to me.
She thinks I'm stupid. But you, she'll listen to you.

CHARLOTTE:
You'd think that would have occurred to her, eh? I
mean, if she's going to do that with one of your
friends, you'd find out sooner or later.

DENISE:
Hey, little brother, you know what you should do,
you should come and live with us. Look at you.
You're skinny as a rail. Your loving sister doesn't
feed you enough. Or was it those Frenchies tried to
starve you to death? Seriously, you could have the front
parlour, we never use it. There's loads of room. You
wouldn't have to worry about us, you could come and
go as you please. And me . . . I'd spoil you rotten . . .

26

SERGE:

Sure, Denise. Have you told Gaston about your little project?

DENISE:

Gaston? Who's Gaston?

LUCIENNE:

I think I have the right to a little respect in my own house.

DENISE:

As if Gaston ever made a decision in his life!

NICOLE:

You went to see the others first, didn't you?

GILBERTE:

All this excitement, it's not good for your father . . . His heart can't take it . . .

CHARLOTTE:

His heart can't stand the strain . . .

NICOLE:

I'm sorry, that was stupid, what I just said. I should know better, you just walked in the door . . . Well . . . Take off your jacket.

DENISE:

You mean I have to eat it all by myself? The whole roast beef? You'll help me with dessert though, eh? A nice piece of sugar pie . . .

SERGE:

You know my soft spot, don't you?

DENISE:

You bet I do!

NICOLE:
Anyway, I think I know why you came here last . . .

SERGE smiles at NICOLE.

CHARLOTTE:
There's Nicole too, we're worried about her . . .

SERGE:
You're always worried about something, aren't you?

GILBERTE:
Well, naturally, we're concerned about all of
you . . . Ever since your mother died, we're the
ones . . .

SERGE:
Aunt Gilberte, that was ten years ago. I'm not
fifteen any more, I'm twenty-five and I'm the
youngest in the family. We're old enough to take
care of ourselves, thank you.

CHARLOTTE:
If we can't even open our mouths . . .

GILBERTE:
How dare you talk to me like that! . . . You have
no right . . .

MONIQUE:
By the way, thanks for sending all your postcards
to the wrong address. It's nice to know that
Madame Proulx downstairs knows more about you
than your own sister.

NICOLE:
It's funny. I just got your last letter this morning . . .

DENISE:
It's a good thing you didn't write me any letters. It
took me three days just to figure out your postcards.

SERGE:
> The one where I told you that after three months I
> finally decided to go see the Louvre?

NICOLE
> No . . . No . . . I didn't get that one yet . . .

DENISE:
> Speaking of postcards, you know those bridges?
> Are they right in the middle of the city or all
> around it like the bridges in Montreal?

SERGE:
> Right in the middle of the city . . .

DENISE:
> Wouldn't you know it, Gaston was right.

NICOLE:
> That means there's one still to come. That'll be
> fun, we can read it together . . .

ARMAND:
> I've got that headache again . . . Hey, Gilberte, you
> got any aspirin?

GILBERTE:
> I don't like it when he gets these headaches.

CHARLOTTE:
> That's three days in a row now . . . Must be the
> excitement, what with you coming home . . .

SERGE: *very loudly*
> Is it any better? Your hearing, is it getting any better?

ARMAND:
> Ah, don't talk about that . . . Forget it . . . Forget it . . .

DENISE:
> So that means Paris isn't on an island . . .

MONIQUE:
> I called home yesterday and Aunt Charlotte answered the phone . . . I thought you were coming back yesterday. Aren't they depressing, those two? I'm so sick of hearing about their illnesses.

LUCIENNE:
> Well, say something!

SERGE:
> You're twenty years older than me, how can I give you advice?

No. 6 Duet

NICOLE:
> It's like . . . it's like waking up after a bad dream. Or as if I'd been locked up somewhere for years without seeing a soul. Before you left, we said that while you were gone we'd think everything over, but the minute you got on the plane, I knew it was all thought out in advance. I love you . . . and I'm ready to face all the . . . problems. If we have to hide for the rest of our lives, we'll hide, that's all. Who knows, maybe someday we won't have to hide any more, like criminals. It's our life, Serge, yours and mine. We mustn't let others spoil it.
>
> *Silence.*
>
> I'd wake up in the morning . . . your place empty beside me, and I'd tell myself, "This can't go on much longer. I won't be able to stand it."

SERGE:
> I know, I couldn't stand it either.

No. 7 Trio

NICOLE:
> When your first letter came and you said you were
> lonely, I must have cried for two days . . .

SERGE:
> I'm the one who wanted to go . . . and boy, did I
> regret it.

LUCIENNE:
> We haven't seen each other for three months and
> you sit there and watch television.

SERGE:
> Why should I tell you about Paris? You never
> wanted to go there, you can't stand the French.

LUCIENNE:
> That's hardly what I want to talk about . . .

SERGE:
> Your affair doesn't interest me. I've already told you.

LUCIENNE:
> Look, I've thought of something . . .

SERGE:
> No, you're not getting me mixed up in this.

LUCIENNE:
> For Godsake, will you listen to me? . . . You can't
> go on living with Nicole. I mean, you just can't do
> that, people are starting to talk . . . And when I say
> people, I mean the family . . . God forbid anyone else
> should find out. Can you imagine the scandal? . . .
> Anyway, I was thinking . . . Are you listening?
> Look, either turn off that damn television or I'll
> smash it. Now, if I were to get you an apartment
> somewhere, like near Carré St-Louis, for instance? . . .

I've seen some nice ones there . . . If I were to rent one for you, you'd have a nice quiet place to live and work . . . and every now and then you could let us use it, me and Robert . . .

No. 8 Solo

ARMAND:
> All I ever wanted in my old age is peace and quiet. Peace and quiet. Haven't I worked hard enough in my life to deserve that? I deserve a peaceful old age.

> *Silence.*

> I deserve it!

> *Silence.*

> Excuse me . . .

No. 9 Duet (Trio Finale)

GILBERTE:
> Well, your aunt can't take any more, she just can't. Enough is enough . . .

CHARLOTTE:
> You couldn't spare your aunty a couple of dollars, could you?

GILBERTE:
> It's her, I can't take her any more. Something's got to change.

CHARLOTTE:
Just two dollars, that's all . . .

GILBERTE:
Stuck in here all day long with . . . with your father whose hearing gets worse every day, and who has no idea what's going on . . . It's not that I don't love him, he's my brother. But he's sick and he won't look after himself . . .

CHARLOTTE:
You see, I haven't received my cheque yet.

GILBERTE:
And her! Her! One of these days you'll find her with a knife in her back, and you'll know who committed the murder!

CHARLOTTE:
Did she tell you not to give me any money?

GILBERTE:
Five years, Serge, five years I've been locked in this house with those two!

CHARLOTTE:
Don't listen to her, she tries to make people believe I'm a thief.

GILBERTE:
For five years I haven't been out of this house, did you know that? It's true! I don't even know where the metro is. I couldn't even find the church on the corner without getting lost. God knows, I'm just as sick as she is, so why is it me who has to do all the work?

CHARLOTTE:
She doesn't believe I'm sick. She says I'm faking.

GILBERTE:
> To sleep in the same room . . .

CHARLOTTE:
> Well, I'm no actress!

GILBERTE:
> . . . in the same bed with a sister you'd like to strangle. You think that's fun?

CHARLOTTE:
> I wish she was in my shoes. That'd shut her up fast!

GILBERTE:
> She hogs the whole bed, snores, like a cow, gets up fifty times a night to pee, coughs and spits for hours on end . . .

CHARLOTTE:
> And you know what else she does?

GILBERTE & CHARLOTTE:
> She phones up the whole family to complain about me.

CHARLOTTE:
> I suppose she thinks I don't know, eh? Well, I'm not that stupid, no sir. I've got the biggest pension and I give the most money, so they'll just have to put up with me.

GILBERTE:
> She's filthy rich, too. She's rolling in it! She gets three cheques at the beginning of each month, and three days later there isn't a penny left. She's spent it all on pills! Oh, they must love her at the drugstore. She's probably keeping them in business. Every year at Christmas I expect them to send her a present, for Godsake.

CHARLOTTE:
It's not very nice to say, Serge, but you know, your father isn't very nice to your Aunt Charlotte either.

GILBERTE:
She takes so many pills, sometimes I think she's in a coma!

CHARLOTTE:
He's always taking her side. They're always against me, the two of them. I don't know what she tells him, but I'm the only one he gets mad at. And I never hear them talking. And I should 'cause if you don't shout, he can't understand. If you ask me, she writes to him!

GILBERTE:
Sometimes I find her on the floor . . . Yes, on the floor beside the bed . . . drugged! I can't pick her up, I'm not strong enough. And if your father's off at the tavern, I just leave her there till he gets back. Then she cries and feels sorry for herself, calls me names. But what am I supposed to do? I'm not going to strain my back trying to lift her!

CHARLOTTE:
Every time I take a pill I have to double check the bottles to make sure she hasn't switched them on purpose . . .

GILBERTE:
You should never have left me alone with them, Serge. When you were here you could talk to them, to her at least . . . She'll listen to you . . . But me . . .

CHARLOTTE:
If aunty promised to give you a little money every month, would you take her to live with you?

GILBERTE:
> No, things have got to change, Serge. Three sick
> people alone in one house, I tell you it's no
> good . . . We can't count on your sisters, they won't
> have anything to do with us. They treat us like old
> rags. After all we've done for them . . . But you, I
> know you wouldn't do that . . . Look, Nicole can
> manage by herself, she's earning a good salary . . .
> Why don't you come back?

CHARLOTTE:
> I wouldn't take up much room, you know. I
> wouldn't make any noise.

GILBERTE:
> If you don't come back . . . Well, they're my own
> flesh and blood, but . . . I might have to leave too.
> I'd feel bad about your father 'cause he can't look
> after himself and he won't go into a home . . .

CHARLOTTE:
> I'd stay out of your way . . . Just a tiny room.

GILBERTE:
> Your room's still there, we never touched it. Your
> Aunty Charlotte wanted to take it, but I wouldn't
> let her . . . 'cause I know you've got a good
> heart . . .

GILBERTE & CHARLOTTE:
> Will you do that for your aunt? Will you?

SERGE:
> I'll think about it, okay? I'll think about it.

GILBERTE:
> But you're not saying no?

SERGE:
> No.

CHARLOTTE:
When will you give me an answer?

GILBERTE:
Your aunt will be waiting for an answer . . .

No. 10 Quartet

SERGE:
I never would have thought . . .

LUCIENNE:
What? That I'd stoop so low? Look, if you're going to preach, don't waste your breath. All I'm asking for is a favour, a simple little favour. It's only 'cause I'm sick of looking for new excuses to get out of the house . . .

SERGE:
And paying for hotel rooms . . .

DENISE:
You won't be shocked, will you, if I take a second helping? I mean, you know me, once a pig always a pig.

LUCIENNE:
Come on. You're always telling me I'm old-fashioned. Between the two of us, I wonder who's worse. You know, I really think . . .

MONIQUE:
Maybe I should take one more pill. I think I'd be okay then . . . Oh don't worry, I won't collapse on you . . . I know when to stop. It's just that I still feel a bit edgy, you know what I mean . . .

DENISE:
For the past few months I've been eating twice what I used to . . . And please, no cracks about my weight, I know I'm fatter. In the time you were gone, little brother, your sister Denise went from large to extra large!

MONIQUE:
Maybe just a half a pill . . . that should do it, eh?

LUCIENNE:
I think that deep down inside you're really shocked.

SERGE:
I just don't want to be the one who has to come along afterwards and clean up your shit.

DENISE:
And the next thing you know . . .

MONIQUE:
Isn't it clever what they do with these pills? Look, they're all marked . . . So, if you only want to take half, or even a quarter . . . Yeah, well, I guess you're not too interested.

LUCIENNE:
Do you think it's any better, your affair with Nicole?

DENISE: *on the verge of tears*
Please everyone, just get off my back and let me enjoy my food. That's all I've got left.

No. 11 Solo

LUCIENNE:
I thought maybe you'd understand . . . After all, your situation isn't exactly normal either, is it? Oh

come on, dear, don't look so surprised. We all know. You can cut the innocent lamb routine, we don't buy it any more. The whole family pretends nothing is wrong, but I wonder what they think when they go to bed at night. No, I saw this coming for a long time. In fact, I even talked to Papa about it years ago. Of course, he didn't want to know, he pretended he couldn't hear me, as usual. Then Denise and Monique, who thought it was so cute that their little brother and sister should love one another like that . . . My God! I don't know how many times I told them it wasn't cute at all. It was sick! But did anyone try to stop it? No, they encouraged you, the whole family. You slept in the same room, and in the morning we'd find you in the same bed. Oh that was fine as long as you were kids, but when Nicole got to be fifteen or sixteen, and you ten or eleven, believe me, it stopped being cute. And what did they do? They just closed their eyes and let it go on. Even when they moved, for Godsake, they still let you share the same bedroom. I only started to breathe again when Nicole left home two years ago . . . I thought it was over, done with. Good Lord, she was twenty-eight and you were twenty-three. It was high time somebody left! But I suppose it was only a lovers' quarrel, eh? Or Nicole just went ahead to prepare your little nest, is that it? Last year, when I heard you were moving in with her, that you dared take that out of the house, I was ashamed, Serge, I was so ashamed! You see, what I'm doing, Serge, isn't sick. You're the ones who are sick! Aren't you ashamed when you look each other in the face? Doesn't that bother you? No, I suppose it gets you all excited, eh? Isn't that it, isn't that how you get your kicks?

Silence.

I bet you couldn't even get it up for a girl who wasn't your own sister!

No. 12 Solo

NICOLE:
> Come over here and sit down . . . It's crazy, but after three months, I feel shy. Like when we were kids and you came back from summer camp . . . You remember? Sometimes it took us a whole week before we could talk to each other.

No. 13 Quintet

LUCIENNE:
> You've got nothing to say. You never thought your big sister could figure all that out, eh? Of course not, you always thought the rest of us were idiots.

SERGE:
> I'm in love with Nicole and Nicole is in love with me. That's all there is to it.

LUCIENNE:
> My God, you can stand there and say it, just like that . . . Could you go and shout it in Papa's ear?

SERGE:
> No, I couldn't. But I'd like to. I'd like to tell him many things . . .

DENISE:
> Excuse me, eh? It's stupid to cry like that. It doesn't do any good, but . . .

SERGE:
> Papa . . .

DENISE:
> Hey, do me a favour and get the pie out of the fridge.

SERGE:
    Papa . . .

DENISE:
    And bring the milk, too . . .

ARMAND:
    What?

SERGE:
    If your hearing aid is broken, you tell me, okay?
    louder   Your hearing aid . . . If it's not working
    right, I'll get it fixed . . . You've got a
    guarantee . . .

ARMAND:
    Don't bother . . . it's not worth it . . .

SERGE:
    Why, it'd just take a couple of days.

ARMAND:
    It's not the hearing aid, it's me. It doesn't help to
    wear it any more.

CHARLOTTE:
    Yes. I was going to tell you, Serge, but I didn't
    know how . . . Your father went to see the
    doctor . . .

SERGE:
    Aunt Charlotte, please! Mind your own business!

ARMAND:
    My headaches kept getting worse, so I went back
    to see them. You know the one I have here . . .
    they don't make them any stronger. This is the
    strongest you can get. That's what they said . . .
    What can you do? . . . If I strain to hear, that's bad
    for me . . . I'm too old, that's all.

No. 14 Quartet

DENISE: *laughing*
And next thing you know, I'll be oversize! That's
what I tell myself when I'm face to face with a
sugar pie. But what can you do, eh? The pie always
wins. I get hypnotized by my sugar pies. Did you
know that, Serge?

SERGE:
What happened to your diet? You were doing fine
when I left . . .

DENISE:
Stay on a diet when little brother's not around to
count my calories? Are you crazy? Besides, you
ought to know I only went on a diet so you'd come
and see me more often . . . I mean, I made you
believe I was on one, but the minute you went out
the door . . .

SERGE:
The sugar pie?

DENISE:
The sugar pie.

LUCIENNE:
So how much longer is this going to go on? When
are you two going to get sensible?

SERGE:
It's going to go on for a long time, I'm afraid.

DENISE:
It's not exactly good for my ulcer, but . . .

SERGE:
Still afraid to have an operation?

DENISE:
Don't mention that word, I'll be sick to my stomach. Oh they say I should have one, but if it's up to me, they'll wait till hell freezes over.

LUCIENNE:
And you say that without batting an eye? I still can't believe it.

SERGE:
Why? It's simple . . .

DENISE:
It's simple, the last time I went in all he took was my blood pressure and I collapsed like a ton of bricks. Crazy, eh? If it takes six of them to hold me down just to get a blood sample, you can imagine what I'd be like on the operating table.

SERGE:
But after it was over you'd be much better off.

DENISE:
I wouldn't be better off after 'cause I'd die during. I know it. Come on, let's talk about something else. I'm losing my appetite.

MONIQUE:
I never see him any more . . .

SERGE:
Huh? What?

MONIQUE:
You never listen when I talk to you! I'm talking about Guy. I said I never see him any more . . . and I'm fed up. If the only reason he wanted kids was so he could dump them in my lap and then beat it, well frankly, he needn't have bothered.

SERGE:
> A salesman has to travel, doesn't he?

MONIQUE:
> Honestly, Serge, you still believe that crap?

SERGE:
> Well, I don't know . . . I hardly know your
> husband . . . He's always so . . . discreet . . .

MONIQUE:
> Yeah, well that's exactly the point. I've had it with
> his discretion. Oh sure, he was always around
> when it was time to make babies. He wouldn't
> have missed that. But where is he now?
> Conventions, meetings, God knows, but he's never
> home. Never. And on top of that, he's stuck me
> with his mother. Well, if that's all my life is, I'd
> just as soon pull out now. No, I'm sure there's
> someone else . . . A woman . . . or women . . .

SERGE:
> Don't start that again . . .

No. 15 Solo

MONIQUE:
> What, you too? You're going to tell me I imagine
> things too? Aren't there enough people doing that
> already? All day long his mother tells me I imagine
> things. When he gets home, I can't say two words,
> he starts screaming I imagine things. Well, I don't
> imagine things and I'm sick of being told I do. Five
> years, five years, I've been taking pills on account
> of my nerves. And for what? To end up listening to
> that crap. You think that's fun? You think that's
> any kind of life? You think I want to end up like
> Aunt Charlotte, a slave to her bloody tranquillizers?

I was really anxious for you to get back . . . I thought you might bring me a little . . . I don't know, a little comfort. But what the hell, I shouldn't ask anyone for anything. That's the first thing we should learn in life, not to ask anyone for anything.

No. 16 Quartet

LUCIENNE:
And what happens if someone finds out? What'll our family look like then?

SERGE:
It won't look any better if they hear about you.

MONIQUE:
I know I'm depressing, but do you think that's fun? Do you think I like being the way I am? Look at me, I'm a nervous wreck. If I had a husband who looked after me I'd be all right, but no, I had to go marry a Jack-in-the-box! You used to come and see me sometimes . . . you'd talk to me . . . But now it seems you have nothing to say . . . You walk in here, you sit down beside me and you stare at the bottom of your coffee cup. Am I really that boring?

SERGE:
Sometimes when I come to see you, you're in no shape to talk.

MONIQUE:
Sure, I know it's all my fault. Look, it's the doctor, our own brother-in-law, who prescribes these pills. What can I do? I have to take them!

DENISE:
If you take the front room like I offered, maybe I'll stick to my diet, a real one . . .

SERGE:
    Promises, promises . . .

MONIQUE:
    Sometimes I'd like to wash my hands of
    everything. The house, the kids, the mother-in-law.
    Wouldn't I love that!

SERGE:
    What would you do?

No. 17 Solo

MONIQUE:
    I'd come knock on your door and ask you to take
    me in, you and Nicole . . . I almost did it when you
    were away . . . In fact, I did do it . . . I got up right
    in the middle of Carol Burnett and I went to see
    Nicole. She'll tell you all about it when you see
    her . . . I spent the night at your place and then in
    the morning I came home. Or, to be more precise,
    I got kicked out. Oh, Nicole was very polite about
    it, you know how she is . . . She reminded me that
    my duty was here, but I know she didn't believe a
    word of it . . . I guess she didn't know how to get
    rid of me . . . Jesus! Another one . . . Oh well,
    what's the difference. I didn't sleep that night
    anyway 'cause I'd gone out of the house without
    my stupid pills.

No. 18 Trio

DENISE: *laughing*
  Why should one sister have you all to herself, eh?
  What about the other three? There's at least one
  who's very plump and very tasty who'd be willing
  to do a lot for you . . .

SERGE:
  I had enough of being passed around when I was a
  kid. I'll decide for myself, thanks.

LUCIENNE:
  Too bad, kiddo, you won't get off that easy.

SERGE:
  Denise, please, no tickling! I'm not a baby any
  more.

DENISE:
  For crying out loud, I haven't seen you for three
  months. Can't I have a little fun?

SERGE:
  Cut it out or I'll leave!

DENISE:
  Good Lord, aren't we getting stuck up! Is that what
  they teach you in Europe? Okay, I get the message.
  From now on I'll admire you from a distance. Just
  give me your picture and I'll set it on the TV . . .
  Good Lord!

LUCIENNE:
  Look, I'm the oldest, so I'm responsible.

SERGE:
  So what are you going to do, tell Papa? It'll kill
  him and you know it.

LUCIENNE:
And what if he finds out from somebody else?

SERGE:
He won't find out if you keep your mouth shut.
Just leave him alone, that's all he wants. And stop
trying to get back at me because I won't run your
whore house.

DENISE:
If I want to see you in person, I'll send you an
engraved invitation imploring you to come.

SERGE:
Denise, you're a drag.

DENISE:
M-m-m- . . . You're so handsome when you're angry.
You make my armpits bristle with excitement!

SERGE: *laughing*
Come on, quit horsing around. We're not kids any
more.

DENISE:
A kiss, a kiss, a kiss . . .

SERGE:
Hey, that tickles, cut it out.

DENISE:
I'd forgotten how good you smell. Oh God, I think
I'm going to faint.

SERGE:
I'm leaving . . .

DENISE:
Surrender! Surrender! Hey, let's play hide and
seek. You hide.

SERGE:
Come on, this is ridiculous. We're acting like a couple of idiots.

DENISE:
No one can see us.

SERGE:
Denise!

DENISE:
Okay, okay. Back to the sugar pie.

SERGE:
Whew! . . . I'm roasting . . . You really scare me sometimes, you know that?

DENISE:
Oh, come on. It's only a joke . . .

No. 19 Quartet

NICOLE:
You look exhausted . . . we ought to go to bed.

DENISE:
It's only a joke . . .

MONIQUE:
Hey, all of a sudden my head's spinning . . . Maybe the pills are too strong.

LUCIENNE:
I won't say anything to Papa . . . But Denise and Monique aren't going to like it, not one bit.

No. 20 Trio

ARMAND:
Serge . . . There's something I want to tell you . . .

GILBERTE:
I'm sick of watching television day in day out . . .

ARMAND:
We never had a good talk, you and me . . .

GILBERTE:
It's always the same . . .

ARMAND:
I can't hear . . . besides, I was always too
embarrassed . . .

CHARLOTTE:
I can hardly stand up any more, but no one ever
believes me . . .

ARMAND:
Down at the tavern I'm always solving the
problems of the world, but when it comes to my
own kids . . . that takes . . . I don't know . . . just
something I never had . . .

GILBERTE:
Always the same . . .

ARMAND:
I guess I was never brought up that way . . .

GILBERTE:
Always the same . . .

ARMAND:
I always felt kind of awkward with you kids, and
maybe I made you the same way . . .

50

GILBERTE:
Even their movies are boring. I've seen them all.

ARMAND:
But there's something I have to tell you . . .

CHARLOTTE:
They want to kill me to get my insurance . . .

ARMAND:
Even if it's kind of hard . . .

CHARLOTTE:
That's what they're after . . .

ARMAND:
There's something . . . I want to thank you for . . .

CHARLOTTE:
It's true, your aunt knows it!

ARMAND:
I wanted to tell you before you left, but I wasn't able to . . .

CHARLOTTE:
Well, they won't get me that easily . . .

ARMAND:
And it's taking about all I've got to tell you now . . .

GILBERTE:
There isn't a movie I haven't seen. There's never anything new . . .

ARMAND:
You remember when you all got together to buy me my first hearing aid . . .

GILBERTE:
> I watch the dumb thing from ten in the morning right through till midnight.

ARMAND:
> That was seven or eight years ago . . .

GILBERTE:
> No wonder I've seen everything . . .

ARMAND:
> I never said anything, I was too proud . . .

CHARLOTTE:
> I'll bury them all.

ARMAND:
> But after I turned sixty and was getting close to retirement . . . and then when I lost my job, I finally gave in . . . I said to myself, all I have left in my life is to try and hear other people . . .

CHARLOTTE:
> They laugh at me now, but you wait. I'll bury them all, one after the other . . .

ARMAND:
> Well . . . I don't know how to describe it, but . . .

GILBERTE:
> There are too many comedy shows, I don't like that either.

ARMAND:
> But the day I got my hearing aid I was scared at first. It was giving me a terrible headache 'cause I'd hardly heard a thing for forty years . . .

GILBERTE:
> They don't make me laugh, those things . . .

ARMAND:
Just the sirens going by, or the vibrations in the floor . . .

GILBERTE:
They're not the least bit funny . . .

ARMAND:
Then, when I came back to the house . . . and I heard your voices, you can't imagine what that did to me . . .

CHARLOTTE:
All Gilberte ever does is say bad things about me . . . But God's going to punish her.

ARMAND:
I didn't know the sound of your voices, my own kids . . .

CHARLOTTE:
And the day I find her lying on the floor, I won't lift a finger . . .

ARMAND:
It was the first time in my life I'd heard you speak . . .

CHARLOTTE:
She'll find out what it's like . . .

ARMAND:
Maybe you don't know it, Serge, but that afternoon you gave me the most beautiful present . . .

CHARLOTTE:
I'll leave her there to die.

ARMAND:
You don't remember what you did?

CHARLOTTE:
Too bad for her.

ARMAND:
Nicole had just bought that new stereo . . .

GILBERTE:
It's like the commercials . . .

ARMAND:
. . . and you took me into the parlour, and you sat
me down in my chair . . .

GILBERTE:
They try to make us believe all kinds of
nonsense . . .

ARMAND:
. . . and you said . . .

GILBERTE:
They think we're stupid . . .

ARMAND:
"Listen to this, Papa!"

GILBERTE:
They can't fool me. I know it's all lies . . .

ARMAND:
Then you put on a record . . .

CHARLOTTE:
I can't wait to see her die.

ARMAND:
I don't remember what it was, I don't know music,
but . . .

CHARLOTTE:
And the rest of them with her.

ARMAND:
    . . . for forty years, Serge, I hadn't heard any
    music.

GILBERTE:
    Oh, Charlotte, stop criticizing!

ARMAND:
    All I ever heard was the loud parts, the fanfares . . .
    But then . . .

CHARLOTTE:
    And what about you with your bloody complaints?

ARMAND:
    To hear the violins, Serge, to hear the violins . . . It
    was like I was in Heaven . . . Goddamn it, like I
    was in Heaven!

CHARLOTTE:
    I long for the day when your mouth will be shut
    for good.

ARMAND:
    It was the most beautiful present . . . the most
    beautiful present in my whole life . . .

GILBERTE:
    And how about me? Don't think I'm not sick of
    listening to you. There are times I wish I was deaf.

ARMAND:
    Now, you can say . . . for once in his life, your old
    man's had a talk with you.

No. 21 Quartet

NICOLE:

Why don't you take a shower before you go to bed? You'll feel better . . .

MONIQUE:

Maybe I'd feel better if I lay down for a bit . . . Come on, let's go into the bedroom . . .

NICOLE:

Get some sleep. We'll talk about it in the morning . . . I mean, we haven't talked about it at all, but we'll try in the morning. I told them at the office I wouldn't be in.

MONIQUE:

When you're here, it doesn't seem so bad . . . I think I even breathe better . . . It's so warm in here . . . Why don't you take off your shirt . . .

DENISE:

There are some things you've got to understand, eh? . . . If I joke with you like this . . .

LUCIENNE:

You were so good then, Serge, so good . . .

MONIQUE:

You can take your shirt off . . . You're not embarrassed in front of me, are you?

LUCIENNE:

I mean, when you were little, you'd listen to me . . .

MONIQUE & LUCIENNE:

I saw you come into the world. I watched you grow up . . .

DENISE:
> You know how I love to have fun . . . But lately,
> whenever I open my mouth . . .

LUCIENNE:
> Remember? . . . You'd do whatever I wanted.

MONIQUE:
> Don't worry, I'm not going to rape you . . .

DENISE:
> You're the only one who isn't ashamed of me . . .

LUCIENNE:
> Sometimes you'd call me your second mama . . .
> Of course Mama didn't like that, but still, it was
> partly true . . .

MONIQUE:
> I just want to look at you . . . Did you never notice
> how I'd look at you when we'd go swimming in
> the summer with the kids?

DENISE:
> It's at the point . . .

MONIQUE:
> It doesn't hurt to look . . .

DENISE:
> It's at the point now . . .

MONIQUE:
> And you're a lot more exciting to look at than my
> boney old husband . . .

DENISE:
> It's at the point now where even Gaston is
> ashamed of me.

MONIQUE:

> We haven't seen each other for three months.
> Surely you could do me this one little favour?

DENISE:

> I mean, seriously, can you believe it? They say I'm
> vulgar!

LUCIENNE:

> Your second mama, eh? Remember that?

MONIQUE:

> Remember when you were little and I used to give
> you your bath? You remember? It was always me
> who gave you your bath. Denise would take you
> out, Lucienne would buy you clothes and stuff you
> full of chocolate, then I got to wash you. And
> Nicole . . . Nicole was forever throwing fits because
> we'd take away her darling little brother. She was
> so cute though . . . Hey, you remember when I'd
> give you your baths together?

LUCIENNE:

> I was the one who really brought you up, not
> Mama. By the time you were born I was already
> twenty. It was me who bought all your clothes . . .
> With my own money too. And boy, did you look
> smart.

MONIQUE:

> There was no hot water in those days. We'd get a
> big kettle boiling on the stove and pour it into the
> cold bath . . . I'd undress you, you and Nicole, then
> I'd put you both in the tub . . . and I'd scrub like
> crazy . . . especially you! . . .

LUCIENNE:

> You remember the white flannel pants you used to
> wear? You were the only kid on the block with a
> pair like that . . .

DENISE:
Everyone used to think I was funny. Remember when you were a kid? Boy, you thought I was a riot.

MONIQUE:
And boy, did you like to get scrubbed.

LUCIENNE:
And I bought baby blue jerseys to go with them.

DENISE:
Of course I gotta admit, I'd do anything to make you laugh.

LUCIENNE:
Remember that? You'd walk around stiff as a board.

MONIQUE:
You'd squirm like a fish . . . a slippery little fish.

NICOLE:
I had it all worked out in my head, everything I wanted to say . . .

MONIQUE:
That's what I used to call you . . .

LUCIENNE:
I used to call you my little soldier. You were proud as hell, even then . . .

DENISE:
Remember when I used to read you "Little Red Riding Hood"?

NICOLE:
But now . . .

DENISE:
> And I'd take out my front teeth and say, "The better to eat you with, my dear."

NICOLE:
> I don't want to talk. I just want to look at you.

DENISE:
> Then you'd stop laughing, eh? . . . You were scared half to death!

LUCIENNE:
> You knew you were good looking then, didn't you? And you know you still are. Come on, say it.

DENISE:
> And I loved to scare you, 'cause then I could grab you all over.

NICOLE:
> I don't know what to do. I'm so happy you're here, then all of a sudden . . .

LUCIENNE:
> Say it.

NICOLE:
> My old fears come back . . . I have the feeling I played with you too much . . . I know we said we wouldn't talk about that any more . . . but . . . I don't want you to feel like a kid with his mother . . .

LUCIENNE:
> You're not as well dressed now as you were then, that's for sure.

MONIQUE:
> It scares me . . . the way . . . I fall asleep like that . . . It's weird.

NICOLE:
Even if it's not my fault . . .

DENISE:
I'd wait for my turn to babysit, then I'd really
scare you. Papa went out on Saturday nights, so we
,all took turns looking after you. We each got to
keep you, one night a month, and did we take
advantage of that!

MONIQUE:
I wish you'd take off your . . .

DENISE:
When my turn came, you were petrified 'cause you
knew I'd hide on you or tell you scary stories . . .

MONIQUE:
Why don't you . . . lie down . . . next to me?

NICOLE:
Honestly, Serge, I never saw this coming!

DENISE:
But you loved it, I know you did.

LUCIENNE:
The money I spent on you!

DENISE:
You loved every minute of it, didn't you?

LUCIENNE:
Your first long pants . . . your first record-
player . . . Hey, that's right, I'd forgotten about
that. I didn't have a cent to my name, but I bought
you your first record-player.

DENISE:
But now . . .

NICOLE:
And I didn't want it to happen!

DENISE:
I have to be satisfied just looking at you.

NICOLE:
It's not our fault, Serge, I know it's not. It's theirs.
They're the ones to blame.

LUCIENNE:
You never thought of that, did you, dear? You still
have a few debts to pay.

DENISE: *very slowly*
"The better to eat you with, you little son-of-a-
bitch." And I'd bite you all over.

No. 22 Solo

DENISE:
But now when I try to be funny, you're the only
one who laughs . . . It's true . . . You know, we've
had the store for five years now . . . We worked
hard to get that place, Gaston and me . . . And we
were happy too . . . Me, I worked the cash, so we'd
save a salary and . . .   *near tears*   Gaston
doesn't want me at the cash any more because he
thinks I'm too fat! He's ashamed of me . . . He . . .
He . . . He gets upset when I'm around! Oh, he
hasn't said so himself, but I can tell, I'm not blind.
You know me, I like to joke with the customers,
eh? I like to laugh . . . and . . . Okay, so I always
talk about my weight, but what do you expect? I'd
rather make jokes about myself in front of people
than have them laugh behind my back. But Gaston
doesn't like it any more. The minute I crack a joke
he gets all huffy. I don't know how to explain it

to you because I don't understand it myself. I'm so worried, I'm so confused, I feel like I'm going crazy. Before, when I'd clown around, he'd be the first to laugh. And he married me 'cause he likes plump women, for Godsake, so what's come over him all of a sudden? Maybe I go too far with my jokes, maybe that's it. *trying to laugh* I don't know. I think it's fun telling dirty jokes to all those prudes and old ladies. Gaston must be afraid of losing customers . . . No . . . No, it's not that. He's ashamed of me, I know it. He's ashamed of me 'cause I'm too fat! Well at least you don't mind, eh, Serge? You don't mind if I'm fat, do you?

No. 23 Solo

SERGE:
You're not fat, Denise. How many times do I have to tell you? It's all in your head. You're the one who keeps saying you're fat. Nobody else thinks so. If you'd only stop talking about it, stop making it the centre of your life. It's all in your head, Denise. You're not fat . . . You're just . . . well, a bit chunky maybe.

No. 24 Solo

LUCIENNE: *slowly*
All I'd have to do is pick up the phone . . . Can you see the look on their faces? I'm sure Monique would swallow a whole bottle of pills . . . And Denise . . .well, when things go badly for Denise, there's always the fridge . . . So, that would make it "official" for all four of us . . . I wonder if we'd

talk about it amongst ourselves or if we'd still try
to keep it hidden . . . One thing's for certain, family
get-togethers would never be the same . . . I can see
it now. Being in that house would be like sitting on
a powder keg. Silences so thick you could cut them
with a knife. You're right though, I won't do it.
There are enough traumas in this family already.
I'm the oldest, the most responsible, so I'll go on
filling Mama's shoes. Someone's got to do it.
Remember what I told you before you left? Maybe
I had to get drunk to say it, but I'm glad I did
'cause I haven't changed my mind.   *laughing*
It's true, Serge. My god, it's true. You should have
been a queer!

No. 25 Duet

LUCIENNE:
You can't imagine how I hoped for that. You can't
imagine. For years I've known that's the best thing
that could happen to you.

NICOLE:
When it happened . . . When I first realized that
when we were together, it wasn't just my little
brother . . . it was a guy, almost a man . . . and that
you were looking at me the way a man looks at a
woman . . . I was so scared. I didn't want it to
happen Serge! I didn't want it!

LUCIENNE:
We used you like such a toy in that house, playing
with you, fussing over you, bringing you up like a
little girl, or rather like a kid with no sex. I could
see it coming . . . With all those women around
you, you'd get screwed up, you'd turn against them
and you'd . . .

NICOLE:
Before that, I never thought it was serious. We were just kids . . . just playing. And the others, they thought it was so cute . . . I was just playing with you, like a kid, that's all!

LUCIENNE: *bursts out laughing*
You know what, Serge? That was your only way out and you didn't take it . . . So all I can say is, too bad for you. Too bad for all of us.

NICOLE:
The first time when you came to me on the sofa and it wasn't just to kiss me good night . . . You were so beautiful, Serge!

LUCIENNE:
'Cause, believe me, you'd be better off with another guy than with your own sister.

NICOLE:
I'd been dreaming about it for a long time, though I'd never admitted it to myself . . . But when it happened . . . it was so frightening and so beautiful . . . that I wished . . . I wished we could both die right there so no one would ever know, ever . . . And mostly so I wouldn't have to remember . . .

LUCIENNE:
I told your friend Robert all about it. Oh, did we have a ball!

NICOLE:
But the next morning we were both alive and things went on as usual. I didn't even feel guilty. You were so happy . . . and so was I.

LUCIENNE:
You know, Robert and I feel the same way about this. He also thinks you're sick.

NICOLE:
Then the second time . . . I didn't think it was ugly or frightening . . . It just made me happy, that's all . . . 'cause it was only natural that it should happen, I guess . . .

LUCIENNE:
Well, as my husband would say, if I could choose my diseases, I'd take the other one. At least then I wouldn't be so ashamed of you.

NICOLE:
And . . . it was beautiful.

No. 26 Solo

SERGE:
Poor Lucienne, to hear you talk, you're the only one in the family with brains. Why do you think I took off for three months? For a vacation? Not with the job I've got. Christ, I had to borrow money to leave because, whether you realize it or not, this is also a big problem for me and Nicole. We've also needed to think about things. Don't forget, I didn't have much choice in this. After all, it was the rest of you who pushed me into it, not knowing, at least I hope not knowing what the hell you were doing. So, here I am, I'm with Nicole, she's thirty and I'm twenty-five. And you can be damned sure I've been asking myself some tough questions. Okay, I'm with her now, but is that really what I want? Am I happy with Nicole? Well, Lucienne, after three months without her, I have to tell you yes, I am happy with Nicole and yes, I'm going to stay with her. I don't care if you're ashamed of me, I don't care if we have to move far away, the point is we're together, and we're going to stay that way for as long as we can. It's clear, it's simple,

and I know what I'm doing. What I feel for Nicole
and what Nicole feels for me is love, Lucienne. It's
love and it's real. It's not a matter of protection or
security, it's love. And it's beautiful. So no one's
going to tell me I don't have the right, because I do
have the right. I have the right to be happy like
anyone else and I'm lucky because I've found my
happiness. Maybe I've found it in my own sister,
but I'm through being ashamed of it. And if the
rest of you lead shitty lives with your shitty husbands
at least have some respect for us, because we're
happy. We're going to live, Lucienne, we're going
to help each other live. And how's this for beautiful?
We're going to live together without hurting one
another . . . I explained all this in my letters to
Nicole and now I can't wait to see her so I can tell
her face to face. And one other thing . . . Don't
bother telling Robert about this, I'll tell him
myself . . . And I bet he'll stop laughing even if
you don't.

No. 27 Solo

NICOLE:
Before I got your first letter, I started to think
you'd forgotten me. Stupid, eh? I told myself
maybe we were right to separate. Maybe now that
he's there he sees he's better off without me.
Maybe after tasting a bit of . . . freedom . . . well,
maybe he doesn't want to come back . . . It's crazy
the stuff you imagine when you're waiting to hear
from someone. A month is a long time. A whole
month with no sign of life from . . . And, I'd
promised I wouldn't write first, that I'd wait, so . . .
by the time your letter came I'd almost given up
hope . . . I came home for lunch one day . . . You
wouldn't believe how I cried, Serge . . . like one of
those stupid French movies we're always laughing

at on TV. You know, when the girl finally gets a letter from her boyfriend, she goes charging all over the house or she flings herself on the bed, bawling her eyes out . . . Well, I did all of that. I did. I was so happy to finally hear from my . . . boyfriend . . . And not only that, you said you were lonely. And you loved me. And you said it was going to be tough, but you'd stick it out for the three months. I'm glad you stayed the three months. Now we know for sure . . . I phoned home right away to tell them I'd heard from you . . . All Aunt Charlotte said was they'd had a telegram when you arrived in Paris, they hadn't heard a word since, that Papa was worried about you . . . and then she hung up. Serge, we've got to do something about Papa. If he's alone with those two much longer, they're going to drive him crazy. Look, I had an idea . . . If you don't like it we won't do it . . . but listen . . .

No. 28 Trio

GILBERTE:
   It gets to the point you don't know what to do any more . . .

SERGE: *very loudly*
   Papa . . .

GILBERTE:
   Roast beef one day . . .

SERGE:
   Can you hear me, Papa?

GILBERTE:
   Chicken or spaghetti the next . . .

SERGE:
I thought about you a lot while I was away . . .

GILBERTE:
Then a roast of veal or maybe a stew . . .

SERGE:
Papa, not once in our lives have we had a serious conversation.

GILBERTE:
And then, you're stuck. You don't know what to do any more.

SERGE:
I hardly know you. And I'm sure you hardly know me.

GILBERTE:
So you go back and start over . . .

SERGE:
When I was a kid, I never saw you 'cause you worked nights, and then later . . .

CHARLOTTE:
Your aunt is sick of eating the same things . . .

SERGE:
Ever since Mama died, you've been escaping to the tavern . . .

CHARLOTTE:
When it comes to cooking, your aunt Gilberte's got no imagination . . .

SERGE:
I don't even know who you are! You never told us!

CHARLOTTE:
I know everything costs a lot . . .

SERGE:
>   Even if your hearing was bad, there were times I
>   needed to talk to you . . . We were the only two
>   men in the house.

GILBERTE:
>   But Good Lord, everything costs a fortune . . .

SERGE:
>   I remember when I was in school. Sometimes I'd
>   write you letters when I needed your advice, but
>   then I'd throw them away 'cause I was too
>   embarrassed to give them to you . . .

GILBERTE:
>   We have a hard time making ends meet, so I can't
>   always fix what I'd like . . .

SERGE:
>   Why was everyone always so embarrassed in this
>   house?

CHARLOTTE:
>   Even if we spent a fortune on food, she'd waste
>   it . . .

SERGE:
>   I mean, we could have learned to use signs or
>   something . . .

GILBERTE:
>   Of course, your aunt's had an awful time with her
>   arthritis . . .

SERGE:
>   Once again, Papa, I have to shout things we'd
>   normally whisper . . . and it's hard.

GILBERTE:
>   Your poor aunt can't even make a pie crust any
>   more . . .

SERGE:
   I realized something terrible while I was thinking
   about you over there.

GILBERTE:
   Say what you like, those ready-made pie crusts
   aren't half as good . . .

SERGE:
   You've never heard us say we love you!

GILBERTE:
   They're like candy . . .

SERGE:
   I know it embarrasses you . . . Don't look away . . .

GILBERTE:
   Nothing but sugar and air.

SERGE:
   Look at me . . .

CHARLOTTE:
   Your aunt tried to make you a real cake for your
   coming home . . .

SERGE:
   I know, you think men don't say these things to
   each other . . .

CHARLOTTE:
   But you should have seen it . . . We had to throw it
   out . . .

SERGE:
   I love you, Papa!

CHARLOTTE:
   Hard as a rock!

SERGE:

It may be twenty years too late, I'm no longer a kid, but I still need to say it. I love you!

GILBERTE:

And your father, he hardly eats a thing these days.

SERGE:

Even if you don't hear, that's no reason not to tell you these things.

GILBERTE:

He pokes around in his plate, but he leaves everything . . .

SERGE:

You can at least read my lips. Papa, I love you!

CHARLOTTE:

She gives him the best parts and he doesn't even touch them!

SERGE:

And if no one's told you so for forty years 'cause it's the sort of thing you don't shout, too bad, I'll shout it. Papa, I love you!

CHARLOTTE:

All I get are scraps . . .

SERGE:

Because I know you need it, you too.

GILBERTE:

It's not even worth trying any more.

SERGE:

Don't cry.

GILBERTE:

It's not worth it . . .

SERGE:
 Papa, please don't cry.

GILBERTE:
 It's not worth the effort . . .

SERGE:
 Don't cry . . .

GILBERTE:
 It's too late to make the effort. It's too late.

No. 29 Octet

NICOLE:
 I know it sounds cruel, but what else can we do?
 We can't leave him there. The others can't take
 him, they all have families. And with us, well . . .
 it wouldn't be long before he realized . . . So I
 thought maybe . . . if we all got together . . .
 perhaps we could put him in a home . . .

SERGE:
 Never! Absolutely never!

NICOLE:
 Some of them are okay, you know.

SERGE:
 Don't ever mention that again, Nicole. Never!

MONIQUE:
 Hey, did I fall asleep? I must have . . . God, these
 pills are strong. How long did I sleep?

SERGE:
 Ten minutes . . . That's all.

MONIQUE:
> You must help me relax 'cause I feel wonderful . . .
> I think I even had a dream . . . I haven't had a
> dream for months. Hey, stay the night, you're good
> for my nerves . . .

SERGE:
> Actually I have to go . . .

NICOLE:
> You want him to stay there?

SERGE:
> No, of course he's got to get out of there . . . I
> never realized it more than tonight . . . Look,
> Denise has an empty parlour . . . she just offered it
> to me . . . She could take Papa . . . And Lucienne's
> looking for an apartment 'cause things aren't too
> hot with Bob . . . And Monique wants out of her
> place . . . Nicole, I want Papa out of there, but he's
> not going into a home. It would kill him.

ARMAND:
> Go on home, Serge, go home and get some
> sleep . . .
> You must be half dead . . .

> *Very long silence.*

SERGE:
> Okay, I guess I'll be on my way . . .

ARMAND:
> Come and see us more often . . .

GILBERTE & CHARLOTTE:
> Your aunt gets lonesome . . .

DENISE:
> Already? Come and see me more often . . .

GILBERTE & CHARLOTTE:
All by herself, day after day . . . with her!

MONIQUE:
You'll come see me more often, won't you?

ARMAND:
I mean, when you feel like it. Don't think you
have to.

DENISE:
It's so nice for me . . .

MONIQUE:
It's so good for me . . .

NICOLE:
But what do we do with the other two?

LUCIENNE:
Serge . . .

DENISE:
And think about my offer, eh? I'm serious . . .

LUCIENNE:
Even if we've argued a bit . . . think about what I
said . . .

MONIQUE:
And if ever you find me on your doorstep, don't
send me away . . .

NICOLE:
They've looked after him for ten years, we can't
just abandon them . . . It's true though, they have
kids of their own . . . Let them take care of them.

ARMAND:
And bring me more books . . . I read all the stuff
you gave me before you left . . . The days are kind
of long . . . That's why I go to the tavern so often.

75

NICOLE:
>Let's go to bed . . . Come on, we'll talk about it in
>the morning. You look like you're ready to
>drop . . .

LUCIENNE:
>Serge . . . Before you go . . . I've thought of
>something else . . .

>*Very long silence.*

>You could take Papa with you . . .   *very fast*
>If you agree, we'll get a big apartment and give
>Papa a room of his own. He'd be better off with
>you than with those two hags . . . Then . . . Robert
>could pretend to come and see you . . . and me
>too . . .

MONIQUE:
>Bye sweetie . . .

DENISE:
>See you, sexy . . .

LUCIENNE:
>Think about it . . .

SERGE:
>Nicole . . . If all else fails . . . Lucienne had a
>suggestion . . .

ARMAND:
>Hey, I forgot to tell you . . . You know Bonnier, my
>buddy down at the tavern? Well, he's got a sister,
>and she saw you in Paris.

GILBERTE:
>Button up good and warm now. Don't let your
>neck get cold.

MONIQUE:
Wrap up warmly . . .

DENISE:
Come on, bundle up . . .

LUCIENNE:
Put up your collar . . .

ALL THE WOMEN EXCEPT FOR NICOLE:
You'll freeze to death!

ARMAND:
She tried to say hello to you, but you were walking
and she was riding in a tourist bus.

CHARLOTTE:
Can you loan me the two dollars?

ARMAND:
She's sure it was you though . . . She wished she
could have talked to you, but . . .

GILBERTE:
Phone me during the week . . .

CHARLOTTE:
Your aunt really needs it . . .

ARMAND:
I mean, she never thought she'd run into someone
she knew in Paris!

Very long silence.

MONIQUE:
Goodbye.

DENISE:
See you.

LUCIENNE:
> So long.

NICOLE:
> Good night.

SERGE:
> Well . . . My taxi . . . My taxi's here . . .

ALL EXCEPT SERGE & NICOLE:
> Bonjour, là! Bonjour!

No. 30 Octet

> *Very rapid.*
> *Long and insistent doorbell.*

GILBERTE:
> My God, you scared me half to death!

CHARLOTTE:
> I thought it was the phone ringing . . .

GILBERTE:
> Is something the matter?

CHARLOTTE:
> I stood there like a donkey yelling into the receiver.

SERGE:
> Is Papa asleep?

GILBERTE:
> It's two o'clock in the morning!

SERGE:
> I want to talk to him . . .

CHARLOTTE:
> That's ridiculous. Come back tomorrow.

SERGE:
> I want to talk to him now!

GILBERTE:
> Are you crazy barging in here at this hour?

CHARLOTTE:
> Is somebody sick?

GILBERTE:
> It's Nicole! Is Nicole sick?

CHARLOTTE:
> Why didn't you phone? It would have been faster.

ARMAND:
> What's going on out here? The whole house is shaking. What are you doing here at this hour?

CHARLOTTE:
> Nicole is sick . . .

ARMAND:
> What?

GILBERTE: *louder*
> Nicole is very sick!

CHARLOTTE:
> Nicole is sick . . .

SERGE:
> Nicole is not sick . . . Nobody's sick!

GILBERTE:
> But you said . . .

SERGE:
> I just said I wanted to talk to my father. You're the ones who . . .

ARMAND:
> What's going on? I can't hear a thing. Speak up!

SERGE:
> I want to talk to you.

ARMAND:
> At three o'clock in the morning?

CHARLOTTE:
> No, it's only two . . .

ARMAND:
> Can't it wait till tomorrow?

SERGE:
> No. *louder* No. I've got to talk to you right away. Otherwise, I might change my mind . . .

MONIQUE:
> Hello, Denise, wait till you hear what's happened!

ARMAND:
> What do you mean, change your mind?

GILBERTE:
> Are you coming home to stay like I asked?

DENISE:
> Eh? What? What's happened? What time is it?

SERGE:
> Papa, I'm going to make you an offer and I want an answer right now.

MONIQUE:
> Lucienne just phoned . . . You won't believe this . . .

CHARLOTTE:
An offer?

ARMAND:
What do you mean, an offer?

SERGE: *almost screaming*
Nicole and I want you to come and live with us!

GILBERTE:
Serge!

CHARLOTTE:
Dear God!

LUCIENNE:
Hello, Nicole? Are you happy now? You've won it all, eh?

MONIQUE:
Papa's moving in with Serge and Nicole.

ARMAND:
Couldn't you wait till morning to ask me that?

DENISE:
But that's crazy. Serge is supposed to move in with us.

SERGE:
I want an answer now! I don't want you to stay here any longer.

GILBERTE:
Sure. Come right out and say it! We torture him!

LUCIENNE:
The least you can do is answer me.

CHARLOTTE:
Is this the thanks we get for looking after him?

NICOLE:
Lucienne, I've nothing to say to you.

DENISE:
When is he going to move?

NICOLE:
Nothing at all.

MONIQUE:
As soon as possible I guess.

GILBERTE:
You're abandoning us!

CHARLOTTE:
Bastard!

NICOLE:
Wait, Lucienne. There is one thing . . . Papa will be fine with us. We'll take good care of him . . .

LUCIENNE:
Degenerate pigs!

MONIQUE:
And do you know what else she tried to make me believe?

NICOLE:
That's right. Good night . . .

MONIQUE:
But it can't be true. It's disgusting!

DENISE:
Coming from her, I'm not surprised. Don't worry, don't believe a word she says . . .

GILBERTE:
What will happen to us?

CHARLOTTE:
Never thought of that, did you? That's not your
problem. You couldn't care less!

SERGE:
Will you shut up!

Silence.

I'm sorry. I didn't mean that . . . But I've got to
talk to my father . . . I know you'll listen anyway,
but please go back to your room. This is between
me and him. I don't want you butting in.

GILBERTE:
Come on, Charlotte.

CHARLOTTE:
We know when we're not wanted.

DENISE:
You'll never get me to believe that, Monique. And
you ought to be ashamed of yourself for even
thinking it.

MONIQUE:
Yes, but if she took the trouble to phone me in the
middle of the night . . .

DENISE:
Goodbye!

MONIQUE:
Hello? Hello?

No. 31 Final Duet

ARMAND:
>Sit down . . . Sit down on the bed . . . You still don't smoke?

SERGE:
>No.

ARMAND:
>That's about my fourth cigarette tonight . . .

SERGE:
>One of these days you'll burn the house down . . .

ARMAND:
>If it hasn't happened yet, it never will . . .

SERGE:
>Yeah, sure.

ARMAND:
>Have you . . . thought about what you're asking me?

SERGE:
>No.

ARMAND:
>The consequences . . .

SERGE:
>I don't care about that . . .

ARMAND:
>Your two aunts . . .

SERGE:
>They've got their own families . . .

ARMAND:
>   And I've got my habits . . . I'm seventy years
>   old . . .

SERGE:
>   Nothing will have to change, Papa. We don't live
>   far away . . . You won't even have to change
>   neighbourhoods . . .

ARMAND:
>   I'm not much good around the house, you
>   know . . .

SERGE:
>   Don't worry about that. That'll work itself out. The
>   important thing is for you to get out of here, and
>   fast.

ARMAND:
>   You're putting quite a load on your shoulders . . .

SERGE:
>   No, I'm not . . .

>   *Silence.*

ARMAND:
>   Serge . . .

SERGE:
>   Yeah?

ARMAND:
>   Serge, if only you knew . . . how long I've waited
>   for this . . . for one of my kids . . .

SERGE:
>   So your answer is yes?

ARMAND:
>   I'll think about it . . . I really will.

SERGE:
Papa . . . There's one other thing . . . It's serious, very serious . . .

ARMAND:
Don't bother about that. I know about that.

SERGE:
You know about it? For how long?

ARMAND:
For a long time. But we won't talk about it now. Your two aunts are listening. Go on home now . . . Go to bed . . .

SERGE:
Yeah, okay. Bonjour là.

ARMAND:
Bonjour.

Fade.